Sex Pleasures

By: Donald A. Peart

7/4/07

ISBN: 0-9702301-4-1

Library of Congress Control Number: 2004091414

Printed in the United States by:
Morris Publishing
3212 East Highway 30
Kearney, NE 68847
1-800-650-7888

Dedication

I dedicate this book to all, especially those who believe they are beyond sexual repair.

Acknowledgment

During the time Judith (my wife) was writing her book *Sexual Healing,* she asked me to also write a complementary book on sexuality. This book is the result. *Sex Pleasures* is not exhaustive relative to sexuality; however, thanks to her for requesting the writing of this book.

Table of Contents

Introduction
(Sex Pleasures)

Healthy sex was intended for procreation and enjoyment. However, sex has become one of the most abused pleasures in life. The pleasure of sex is so intensively pursued that mankind risks disease from sexuality. Sex pleasure is the cause of so many hurts to humankind.

In ancient Greece, it was customary for adult male to pursue young boy slaves to have sex with these defenseless victims. (The Greek god Zeus is known for stealing one of these young men for his own pleasure.) Can you imagine the terror that these boys felt as these grown men chased them? Today men and women alike are raped by abusive people, all for sex pleasure.

Sex pleasure which was given for value by the Creator is now devalued for the apparent ecstasy of climax. The indulgers do not understand the implication of abused sex, nor the apparent pleasure that is being experienced. Do you the reader know sex is one of the pleasures of the Garden of Eden? There is value in sex, and abused sex causes devalue of the body.

This book will look at some aspects of sex-pleasures, including a look at the history of humankind as it relates to sex. It is intended to help the reader (male/female) see the value of healthy sex. This book also speaks to that which is sexually unhealthy. May this synoptic text begin the healing process for those who really desire sexual repair!

Blood Sex

The hymen in women has stymied mankind for a long time. What is its purpose? It breaks during intercourse and causes bleeding—Blood sex.

A definition of this form of sex (blood sex) is found in the historical culture of Greece. Let us take a synoptic look at the etymology of the word *hymen*. Hymen is the Greek god of marriage.

Thus, the hymen points to something that should only be made to bleed at the consummation of a marriage. The answer that has eluded mankind for so long is found in the history of the word *hymen*. The hymen is to be broken only at marriage. This is what I call, blood sex.

It has been difficult for some to find out the reason for the hymen. To them, it served no purpose. In their intellect they were dumbfounded. The hymen only breaks when the virginity of a woman is ended. The answer is found in the function of the women relative to the man. The purpose of the hymen is for blood covenant, through blood sex within the confines of marriage.

Marriage is sometimes referred to as "wedlock." The participants are "locked" during/after the wedding. The reality is that wedlock is permanent, because "Until death do us part" has meaning. When people get divorced, there is a kind of death, death to a marriage. The vows of wedlock were covenanted with "until death do us part" and consummated in blood, even if the wife's hymen has already been penetrated. For those who understand the history of blood covenant, the breaker of the covenant must die.

Blood sex takes on a whole new meaning now. Whenever a man and a women decide to have blood sex (breaking virginity), there is a "binding" associated with it. Covenant in some cultures is always associated with blood—from cutting of a finger to the killing of animals. The Hebrew concept of covenant is to cut flesh in two pieces so as to let blood flow, and then to walk through the two pieces of flesh.

The woman and the man make covenant the same way. She is designed to have an opening. The male then passes between the two pieces of flesh, breaking the hymen (blood sex). Thus the covenant flesh is cut. One of the Hebrew words for female means to puncture. At the puncture, blood flows to create the covenant. It is also a known fact that every time there is sexual intercourse, blood flows in the lubricant produced by the body of the woman. This means that blood covenant is constantly being reinforced. This is why it was said earlier that even if a person is not a virgin at marriage, a covenant is still cut in the marriage bed.

This covenant of blood sex is binding. This is why when a virgin is penetrated by a male, there is a natural attachment. The covenant has been cut. Sometimes when couples get married, they may think about other sex partners as they are having sex with their real partners by marriage.

That is, every other sex partner, before marriage, is also a blood covenant partner. Those sex-covenants have to be denounced, and cut off by the most powerful Blood— the Blood of Jesus. Dissatisfaction comes in marriages because of the other blood covenants that were cut. The heart, by nature, seeks out every covenant. Believe it or not, blood is a "will." This is why it is so hard to break the covenant (the will) set by blood.

Allow me to tell you the profoundness of blood sex as it relates to satanic worshipers. You may be one reading this book. Part of the initiation of the woman is that the satanic high priest rapes the woman who wants to join that cult. The initiation is then consummated by the drinking of the blood of the human sacrifice in some cults.

This is why it is such a difficult task to rescue satanic worshipers. Forbidden blood covenant, and perverted blood sex is involved. The satanic high priest binds the person to Satan's sexuality by blood. The person then goes further by drinking blood. Even the dark world knows the power of blood.

Mankind was created only to have one blood covenant partner. Blood sex is to be with one person (a spouse), not with many partners. There is a joining when sex is accomplished. If a person has sex with a prostitute— prostitute sex—that person becomes one with that prostitute. Some blood covenant gets a little extreme....

Anal sex is also a filthy covenant. Remember, I said covenant has to do with passing between two pieces of flesh. Thus, if a man passes between the two pieces of the flesh of the "anus" of another man, a forbidden covenant is being cut. It is a covenant of dishonor. This covenant of dishonor is why it is so difficult for men to get out of homosexual relationships, and the relationships are always filled with dishonor. Thus, as indicated, a covenant is also cut by these acts of "anal sex."

Women who have sex with other women are also creating a covenant with other women. This is also confuses sex. I am reminded of an event my mother related to me. She met a young lady at a mall. The girl wanted to talk to someone. (I guess my mother looked motherly.) The young girl had apparently gone out with a co-worker/friend to a party. The young girl eventually gets raped by this other woman at the party. The female rapist tore the young girl physically, and devastated her emotionally. She indicated to my mother how she was confused. She did not know if she was "straight" or "gay". The woman of lesbian orientation tore up the insides of the naive young lady, causing blood to flow. Thus, the victim went away confused as to her sexual orientation. A sick mind makes covenant with the same sex, willingly or unwillingly. A sick mind cut covenant with multiple partners. Blood sex is very significant. It is not to be abused.

Vagina means "sheath" as in a sheath for a sword, the actual Latin meaning for the word. The vagina coupled with the hymen is made for the sword of a male. The vagina was not designed for manmade sexual devices used by male and female. The "anus" was made to release gases and excretions from the large intestine or colon. It was not made to receive the penis. The "sword" does not fit. Anal sex will only damage the anus, and the bleeding that occurs only compounds the problem of breaking away from such perversion. Stop trying to make the penis fit. It is only destroying the body. Anal sex is wrong covenant.

Women you were created for blood sex. You were created to be one of the couple who 'lock' the marriage. Men, you were created for blood sex. You were made to use the "sword" to cut the hymen and initiate the covenant in a right and permissible manner.

The hymen is for covenant; and blood sex is for marriage ….

5

Mind sex

Mind sex—it has been happening for millenniums. Today, we call it wet-dreams.

Sex in the mind began with angels millenniums ago. Everything has a beginning, and there are spiritual beings called *"beginnings."* Some call them *"principalities," "angels that fell,"* or *"sons of God."* They are called beginnings, because they are initiators of things that did not exist before they started these particular things. Some of these "sons of God" introduced humanity to mind sex.

The book of **Genesis** (Greek for **beginning**) documents many beginnings. One of these is sex in the mind. Mind sex had its beginning in the early days of mankind. Men began to birth beautiful daughters. This happened as humans populated the earth. The beauty of these daughters must have been significant, because it was specifically documented.

The problem concerning these beautiful women was angels could also see their beauty. Before Adam and Eve, mankind as we know it now, did not exist on the earth. Thus, the beauty in women was also seen by the angels for the first time.

This beauty in women led the angels to hold a desire for the women's beauty, and all the accoutrements that God placed on and in women. Thus, there was a great "taking" of the women by the angel in order to have sex with them. The beginnings began their rebellion in the minds of women. The manifestation came as these beings from the unseen began to show themselves in the minds of women.

The encounter became so real that womankind began to partake also. The trap of this acceptance of the angel by the women is that they were seized by the invisible. (I will develop this point in a moment.) Thus, they became the very thing that they had pleasure in. These are some of the same entities that come to the minds of men and women today in which both men and women have what we call wet dreams. With that said, let us look at some historical facts concerning mind sex.

Genesis 6:1-3, NKJV:
*[1]Now it came to pass, when men began to multiply on the face of the earth, and daughters were born to them, [2] that the sons of God saw the daughters of men, that they were beautiful; and they **took** wives for themselves of all whom they **chose.***

The first word of discovery in the historical text above is the word **"took."** Mankind has been baffled by these appearances of beings in their sleep. People call them soul mates today. Some call them incubi and succubi. How did they come into being? Some of these beings are women who were **taken** to that unearthly realm, never to live physically in the natural again.

7

"Took" is translated in the Hebrew as *laqach (law-kakh'),* which means "to take," according to Strong's Concordance. An interesting word is **derived** from this word (laqach). It is *leqach (leh'-kakh).* This derivative is translated as "doctrine" and "learning." Strong's Concordance also states that this word carries the idea of giving or receiving **mental instruction.** This is how mind sex started.

First, let us understand that the "sons of God," as stated before, are also called angels and principalities (beginnings). This is important. The "sons of God" in the text above are not men. They are spiritual entities. The historian Jude, along with *Genesis 6:4,* provided the link.

Jude 6-7, NKJV:
[6] *And the **angels** who did not keep their **proper domain (lit., principality or beginning),** but left their own **abode (lit., residence),** He has reserved in everlasting chains under darkness for the judgment of the great day;* [7] ***as** Sodom and Gomorrah, and the cities around them in a similar manner to these, having given themselves over to sexual immorality **and gone after strange (Gk., hetéras, Eng., different) flesh,** are set forth as an example, suffering the vengeance of eternal fire.*

These "angels" went after "strange or different flesh"— the different flesh of women. In other words, angels do not have flesh or bodies as we know. Thus, the flesh of these women was different from theirs *(compare 1 Corinthians 15:40)*. The angels did not keep their beginning. Thus, they began another beginning. They slept with the daughters of mankind. These angels are called the *"sons of God"* in Genesis 6.

These angels **"took** wives for themselves of all whom they **chose."** As we learn above, "took" has the idea of mental instruction. The angels did not approach the women haphazardly. In the same manner these incubi and succubi that visit people in their dreams and mind today, do not entice the mind of humanity for no reason.

They first get familiar with a person in dreams over a period of time. This is also seen in Genesis 6:2. The word **"chose,"** properly means **"to try"** according to Strong's lexicon. This is a significant discovery which gives insight into the approach of these angels towards women. The idea of "trying" is that the spirit beings would **"try"** the women and the ones who submitted to their enticement were the ones the angel would **"choose."**

Now note: Just like these types of sexual encounters in the dreams of some today have a form of pleasure to the flesh of the indulgers; so, likewise, there were forms of pleasure for those whose minds were enticed by the angels. Remember, the word "took" has in it the idea of "mental instruction."

Thus the angels kept "trying" by "mental instruction." It was a constant approach by the spirits to create familiarity. All the women that accepted the pleasure of sex in the mind were then "taken" to the realm of the invisible, literally. This is a key to understanding how there are female spirits who can appear in dreams.

The word "took" carries the idea of being transported from one dimension to another, from the natural to the spiritual. To prove this, let us look at another historical fact that occurred **in the same period** that the women were **"taken."**

Genesis 5:24, NKJV:
And Enoch walked with God; and he was not, for God ***took*** *him.*

Hebrews 11:5, NKJV:
*By faith Enoch was **taken away** so **that he did not see death,** "and was not found, because God had taken him"; for before **he was taken** he had this testimony, that he pleased God.*

Enoch was so taken that he should not see death, because God **"took"** him. This is very interesting. Enoch was taken to the point of not existing in this realm anymore. The Bible History says, *"He was not, for God took him."* In order to understand the full weight of what it means that the sons of God *"took wives for themselves,"* one must also see the word "took" as it applies to Enoch.

This word "took" was used in the same context of history, the period just before the flood. Enoch was a man from the earth realm who was "taken" to the realm of God—the unseen. God, who is Spirit, *"took" him."* The angels did the same to those women who submitted to the spirits' sexual approach in their mind. The angels, who are spirits, ***"took wives*** *for themselves."* Do you see it?

Another way of saying this is that the women who were "tried" by the angels and subsequently chosen were taken to the dimension of the invisible by these angels. Thus, these women became succubi. The transport became permanent. God took Enoch "so that he did not see death." In like manner, these beautiful daughters of mankind were taken as wives to the dimension of the invisible never to see natural death. (However, there is a second death).

They now live on through the ages never to see death until God purges them from the earth. These succubi now seduce mankind in their dreams. This form of mind sex is now accepted in society as normal. However, these kind of sexual encounters with succubi are the catalyst for quick ejaculation in men and quick climax in women (relative to incubus). Let me explain.

The Jewish historian Jude stated that *"these **dreamers** defile the flesh" (Jude 8)*. The word "dreamers" is from a Greek word that literally means, "that which is **seen** in the sleep." In the context of this statement of Jude, he was referring to sexual sins. These sex sins came from mind sex. It was seen in their minds while sleeping. Jude then said that this type of mind sex *"defiles the flesh."*

Mind sex affects the flesh. This kind of sex is so climatic that people prefer it (mind sex) to the real thing (real sex). This kind of mind sex stunts real sex. The practicality of this is that there are a lot of people who cannot enjoy sex unless they get kinky or weird. The level of excitement with real sex is not enough. Sex in the mind, relative to things seen in dreams, in the process of having real sex is the only thing that drives certain sex pleasures.

This kind of sex (mind sex) is so defiling that the defiled flesh of the indulger can rub off on garments and people (Jude 23). For example, a pure person happens to hook up with a person who indulges in mind sex; eventually, that person may starts indulging in all kind of illicit sex. That person's flesh was defiled through the flesh of the "dreamer." Some people are possessed with succubi and incubi. Therefore, there are people who are having sex with demon-like entities in people.

Mind sex may contemplate pleasure, but there is a judgment (not necessarily future) to every pleasure ....

Angel sex

Angel sex—what are the unwanted results of the angels (incubi, succubi) having sex with humankind?

Humans were not made to destroy each other. However, through the ages fallen angels have caused humanity to kill each other. This is seen in history relative to abortion. The practice of abortion is a direct result of sex with spirits. I call sex with spirits "angel sex." A sick mind can look at someone who looks just like him/her and then kill that person. There must be an explanation. It is called history, from the perspective of the One with all knowledge. Again, everything has a historical beginning.

The Creator was so generous that He employed a specific people to record certain portions history for us. History did not start with the Greeks. History started with the Creator. His record in Genesis states: *"This is the **history** of the heavens and the earth when they were created ..." (Genesis 2:4, NKJV)*. He "created" (started the beginning), thus he can give historical facts about any beginning, and even the beginning of angel sex, and His record is true.

Genesis 6:4, NKJV
*There were giants on the earth in those days, and also afterward, when the sons of God came in to the daughters of men and they **bore** children to them. Those*

*were the mighty men who were of **old (lit., concealed),** men of renown.*

These sons of God are angels, as stated earlier in this book. The text above also called them "mighty men who were of **"old."** As indicated above, **"old"** is the Hebrew word that means "concealed" according to Strong's Concordance. Let us take a second look at the Scripture with the word "concealed" inserted. "Those were mighty men who were of "the 'concealed,' men of renown."

These sons of God were from the concealed. They came from the invisible (concealed) for the express purpose of sleeping with the beautiful daughters of mankind; and, believe it or not, angel sex can produce babies. Allow me to prove it.

Angels are spirits right? The answer is clearly "yes" (Hebrews 1:13-14)! Most of the people who follow Christianity all believe in the virgin birth of Jesus. This is an accepted fact in most of the western world. History, again, records for us how this virgin birth took place.

Matthew 1:18, NKJV:
*Now the birth of Jesus Christ was as follows: After His mother Mary was betrothed to Joseph, before they came together, **she was found with child of the Holy Spirit.***

Note: It was the Spirit that caused this "woman" to be "found with child. The Book teaches that it was the **Holy Spirit** who "procreated" the Child in Mary. As stated before, angels are spirits, and spirits have the ability to impregnate women. People who deny that spirits can have babies deny the Immaculate Conception. This is the reason why mind sex and angel sex is so dangerous. This is the deception; if you believe that conception is not possible, then you will be open to angel sex. Fallen Angels are still trying to impregnate women. There is also a twist to this for the men.

When the succubus comes to you in your dream and you find yourself having ejaculations in your sleep in that spirit being, it is actually trying to reverse the process. That is, it is trying to give life to your sperm. You may think this concept is extreme. Christ said that at the end of days men will be doing the same things as were done in the days of Noah (Matthew 24). Angel sex began in the days of Noah. Sex with angels was one of the primary reasons why God destroyed the earth with a flood. Per the history book, the Bible, **"violence"** was a direct result of angel sex.

> ### Genesis 6:1-11, NKJV:
> [1] *Now it came to pass, when men began to multiply on the face of the earth, and daughters were born to them,* [2] ***that the sons of God saw the daughters of men, that they were beautiful; and they took wives for themselves of all whom they chose.*** [3] *And the LORD said, "My Spirit shall not*

strive with man forever, for he is indeed flesh; yet his days shall be one hundred and twenty years."
⁴ There were giants on the earth in those days, and also afterward, when the sons of God came in to the daughters of men and they bore children to them. Those were the mighty men who were of old, men of renown. ⁵ Then the LORD saw that the wickedness of man was great in the earth, and that every intent of the thoughts of his heart was only evil continually. ⁶And the LORD was sorry that He had made man on the earth, and He was grieved in His heart. 7 So the LORD said, "I will destroy man whom I have created from the face of the earth, both man and beast, creeping thing and birds of the air, for I am sorry that I have made them." ⁸But Noah found grace in the eyes of the LORD. ⁹ This is the genealogy of Noah. Noah was a just man, perfect in his generations. Noah walked with God. ¹⁰And Noah begot three sons: Shem, Ham, and Japheth. ¹¹The earth also was corrupt before God, and the earth was filled with **violence.**

This record of **violence** was made in the context of angel sleeping with humanity—Genesis 6:1-4. Sex with spirit beings was never intended by the Creator. There is violence related to angels mixing with mankind in a certain way. Dreams of having sex with a so called soul-mate are not happpenstance!

It is a deliberate result of angels cohabiting with men and women. The result is always violence. I read an article recently concerning an officer in the military who killed his wife because pornography (The Sun: Tuesday, Oct1, 2003, page 5B). There exists violence, fueled by perverted sexuality that manifests itself in many ways.

Beating during sex is a sign that angel sex is being indulged in by at least one of the parties involved. Biting during sex is also a result of sexual encounters with angels. Pornography (i.e. perverted sex acts in print, the media, and websites) is the source of many serial killer homicides. Watching naked people having sex (pornography) is a result of what was seen through mind sex. Those vivid pictures that occur during mind sex or angel sex are the originators of pornography. People produce the very images they see in their minds. These images can come through sex pictures and dreams. How many times have you acted out (taken on the image) of a sex movie or picture you have seen?

The result of angel sex has been detrimental to humankind. It resulted in hatred for their kind. This is the reason why men degrade women. Mankind has exposed women and men to the same treatment the fallen angels initiated. **There is a dark violence associated with angel sex**. Evil angels perverted everything that is related to human sexuality, to the point of teaching us abortion. In the text above "the sons of God" produced babies with the women of the earth. The women **"bore** children to them."

The phrase **"bore children"** in the Hebrew also means **"to be a midwife."** Not only did the women that slept with the angels have their babies, the angels also were the **midwives** to these women. This is very significant, because the word "giants" means "fallen ones." The word giant is from the same root word that abortion or untimely birth is derived from. Yes, there were giants. However, there were also abortions.

The angels who were midwives to the daughters of men taught mankind how to kill—abort—their own babies. The fallen ones were untimely births. They were not to be born at the appointed time. The fallen ones are abortions from the mixture of angels' having sex with women; and, the angels also aborted babies. Finally, the angels aborted babies. They became the midwives of death for babies that were not wanted. This was and still is a direct result of angel sex. If you have aborted, ask the Creator to forgive you. He will.

Now, there are a lot of people who do not believe that angel sex will ever happen again. This is not true. History sometimes repeats itself to a degree. When the **first set** of angels sinned and slept with women, they were locked up until the Day of Judgment, according to the historian Jude (.Jude 6). However, history gave us a glimpse into the future, indicting that the same thing happened again.

Genesis 6:4, NKJV
*There were giants on the earth in those days, **and also
afterward,** when the sons of God came in to the
daughters of men and they bore children to them. Those
were the mighty men who were of old, men of renown.*

This exact record of earliest history tells us that giants
were in the earth in the days of Noah **"and also
afterward."** This indicates to me that other angels did
the same thing the first set did. They instituted angel sex
again. Listen to the Holy writ—*"**and also afterward
when** the sons of God came in to the daughters of men
and they bore children to them."*

The proof that giant beings were born in the earth again
is when Moses, Joshua and Caleb went to possess the
land they also encountered "giants"—children of the
cohabitation between mankind and fallen angels. The
most trusted prophetic historian also said something
similar: *[26] **And as it was in the days of Noah, so it will
be also in the days of the Son of Man:** [27] They ate, they
drank, they married wives, **they were given in marriage,**
until the day that Noah entered the ark, and the flood
came and destroyed them all"* (Luke 17:26-28, NKJV).

The end of days will be like the days of Noah. Men and
woman will be sleeping with spirits again. According to
Genesis 6, angels married and slept with women. Jesus
says, "They were given in marriage." The same thing is
happening today.

Men and women are cohabiting with spirit beings. I was told by a young lady who is dating a Mason, how he had sex with her without touching her physically. She felt the reality of it, but it was not physical. This is a manifestation of spirits sleeping with men and women.

I am going to make a bold statement. Angel sex is or will again produce children in the natural realm. The day will declare it ....

Anal sex

Anal sex—it has become one of the pleasures of sexuality. To a lot of men and women anal sex is now a norm.

In the mind of today's world, pleasures of sex in any form are widely accepted. Anal sex is among the many pleasures. What could be wrong with this kind of sex? A young lady was counseled by Judy (my wife) some time ago. The young lady happened to be a Jehovah's Witness.

She informed Judy that she and her husband regularly indulged in anal sex. The young lady finished the conversation by saying that her husband preferred anal sex to conventional sex. The young lady also indicated that she did not intend to give up anal sex either. This appears to be the norm today. However, there is something wrong with this kind of behavior in humanity. It should not be the norm.

The origin of anal sex is again from the principalities of beginnings who initiated this behavior in mankind. Again, we must look at history. Most cite Sodom as the origin of anal sex. However, the first indication of this kind of behavior goes back to the days of Enoch and Noah. It was in Noah's day that the first set of angels fell (left their proper domain) for the daughters of Adam.

Jude 6-7, NKJV:

[6] And the angels who did not keep their proper domain, but left their own abode, He has reserved in everlasting chains under darkness for the judgment of the great day; [7] **as** *Sodom and Gomorrah, and the cities around them in a similar manner to these, having given themselves over to sexual immorality and* **gone after strange flesh,** *are set forth as an example, suffering the vengeance of eternal fire.*

For a true appreciation of the reality of angel sex with humanity, one must be able to see the conditions of the beginning of their contempt of the law of the Creator. What I mean is this: Man and woman humankind did not exist before Adam and Eve. Thus, there must have been some interest in this creation of man and woman.

The angel saw man and woman in their nakedness. This awareness began in Eden and continued to the time when angels had sex with the women. The beauty of the flesh of womankind aroused their curiosity. Angels by nature appear to be nosey. They like *"to look into"* things. *(1 Peter 1:12).* They were so infatuated with the beauty of women, they wanted to defile them. I believe these angels wanted to experience the "eden" of sex. Thus, the fallen angels began in humanity many sexual acts that were invented by the fallen angels.

Anal sex originates with angels. Listen again to the historian, Jude: *"The angels who did not keep their proper domain, but left their own abode ...* **as** *Sodom*

22

*and Gomorrah ... having given themselves over to sexual immorality and **gone after** strange flesh" (Jude 6-7, NJKV).*

The word **"after"** is very significant. The Greek is **"opísoo"** which literally means **"to the back."** **"Gone"** is also of importance. The Greek also carries the idea of **"behind."** These two words have a lot of implications. Especially, in light of the statement, *"as Sodom and Gomorrah ..."* Sodom and Gomorrah were noted for anal sex. It was so bad in those cities that the men of Sodom even tried to have sex with a couple of the elect angels as we will see shortly.

Anal sex was enacted by "principality (lit., beginning)" angels. They initiated this in human behavior with women. The spirits were the first to approach women and men from behind, **"as"** in Sodom. They were the first to go **"to the back"** of the women and men **"as"** Sodom and Gomorrah. Thus, from this historical fact we see that anal sex began in the days of Noah **"as"** anal sex was also performed in Sodom. Maybe it is a little clearer now as to why the Creator destroyed humanity.

The heart of humanity became so corrupt by perversion that their heart diffused evil all day *(research the Hebrew words in Genesis 6:5)*. When succubus and incubus appear in your dreams to indulge in anal sex, it is time to resist. It is an act that was developed to trap humanity for the angel's pleasures. This so called mind pleasure is then transmitted to humanity in many forms—one of which is pornography. Anal sex is propagated in humankind by porno distribution. The angels and humankind gave *"themselves over to **sexual immorality (Greek; ekporneuo)** and gone after **strange flesh."***

"Ekporneou" literally means, "ek" ("out of") and "porneu" ("the act of porno"). Once a human being gives himself/herself over to the act of pornography the next involuntary stem is anal sex. It was "out of the act of porno" that "strange flesh" was "gone after" (to go to the back from behind) by angels and mankind. Sex in the "behind" is "strange flesh." Sex was meant to be with the female sex organ not with the anus—the feces organ. The anus is strange flesh to the penis.

The result of pornography will be sex with strange flesh, to include but not limited to, men having sex with men. Man in man is having sex with strange flesh. Woman having sex with woman also is "strange flesh." Man involved in anal sex with woman is also sex with strange flesh. Men with animals and women with animals are also in the category of sex with strange flesh. According to the historian Jude, anal sex has its origin out of the act of pornography. The more humankind act out what they see in their dreams and in movies, the more the land will be defiled with the act of anal sex.

In my first statement in this section, I stated how anal sex is now preferred over conventional sex. This was also true in early history. The setting was Sodom and Gomorrah.

In the history of Sodom and Gomorrah, we learn that Lot's daughters had married. The record stated that he had sons-in-law *(Genesis 19:14)*. However, the text also called Lot's daughters virgins—*"who have not known a man" (Genesis 19:8)*. This seemed contradictory. They were married, yet, they were virgins. In those days marriage was consummated with sex. However, what kind of sex consummated the daughters of Lot's marriages? An implicit answer is anal sex. The husbands of these daughters preferred anal sex over conventional sex. Let us investigate. When the angels came to the city of Sodom to destroy it, they were approached by *"the **men** of Sodom, both old and young, **all the people from every quarter" (Genesis 19:4).***

"All" the people included Lot's sons-in-law, because the text said "**all** the people." The text also stated that these "**men** of Sodom" came from "**every** quarter." Thus we can see that Lot's sons-in-law were indulgers of anal sex. The men of the city wanted to have sex with the male angels. These angels were men *(Genesis 19:5)*. With what part of the body were they planning on having sex? To put it quite vividly, the men of Sodom wanted to have sex in the "behind" of the angels. This is a demonstration of men's mind in a very sick state— trying to have sex with the elect angels of the living God.

This awful fact now leads to my point. Lot's sons-in-law probably did consummate their marriage. They preferred anal sex over conventional sex. Yes, even though Lot's daughters did not know man. "Not knowing a man" may refer to conventional sex. To prove that Lot's sons-in-law's unconventional sexual habits had defiled his daughters and that his daughters may have been tainted with the sex of strange flesh, let us look at what Jude taught again. They were "defiled" as Jude had taught, by the "flesh" of their husband *(Jude 8)*. This is the proof.

After the cities that were involved in anal sex were destroyed, they got their father drunk and slept with him, bearing children. Sleeping with their father was sleeping with "strange flesh." We call this incest. (I would like to make a note here: even though the children of this union were from incest, God allowed one of the children to be in the lineage of Jesus. Thus, there is strong consolation for those who are born from incest. God is still in your corner *(compare Exodus 6:20))*.

However, let us get back to the aim of this section, addressing the preference of anal sex <u>in lieu</u> of conventional sex. Lot's sons-in-law preferred anal sex. They were partakers with the men of the city who would rather have sex with men. In our days, there are men who go up to seven months without conventional sex with their wives, because they are involved in anal sex with other men. It is abnormal for a man not to desire a woman.

There are men who cannot have sex unless anal sex is involved. This is the work of the succubi and incubi. There is no "rise" for the man or excitement in the woman unless a sexual vice is involved. Succubi and incubi have desensitized humanity with respect to conventional sex. The norm is now to be married, yet have a "fling" on the side. The male in the marriage has a male fling; the female in the marriage has a female fling on the side. This is infirmity of the mind demonstrated.

The warning is: this kind of action must be addressed, and people must change their mindset concerning this unclean act. Sodom and the surrounding cities were destroyed for anal sex. Sodom had time to be "idle" among other things which resulted in doing "abominations"—disgusting acts *(Ezekiel 16:49-50).* The result was destruction. The same is true for the cities of today. Bad things will happen and are happening because of the practice of anal sex.

The pleasure of anal sex is temporary, but the misuse of the body has eternal implications.....

Prostitute sex

Sex is so valuable that men pay money for it— Prostitute sex. However, those who give sex without cost are worse than strumpets—what then is Prostitute sex?

Historically speaking, a prostitute was always a woman/man who allowed the use of his/her sex organs for a price. This fact is definitely true, but not complete. I learned that a woman who gives the use of her body for sexual pleasure freely is worse than a strumpet. At least, the strumpets get paid for their service. Prostitute sex takes on a new meaning altogether.

Now, I am not advocating the selling of sex. Giving sex freely and selling sex are equally considered prostitute sex. Prostitution has an origin, and history is the place where we can find the source. This time we look to another trusted historian a disciple called John. According to John, prostitute sex is associated with an entity called *"Mystery Babylon."* Who is this Mystery Babylon?

First, realize that Mystery Babylon is a spiritual entity that manifests itself through mankind. Second, we will look at prostitute sex as defined by the Greeks. What I mean is this: the words harlot or prostitute is derived form the Greek words "pornos" and/or "porne." From these words we get our English word porno and pornography. In Greek culture, fornicators (porne or pornos) were those who sold their body for sex. In fact, the words pornos or porne is derived from a root word which means "to sell."

However, as demonstrated in the first three sections, we see that there is a spiritual source of perverted sexuality in humanity today. Did you know that humanity is created to house the Holy Spirit? However, instead we have become houses of all kind of other spirits—even the spirit of prostitute sex.

There is this great prostitute that can only be described spiritually. A lot of people run from "spirituality", but the soul mates they see during mind sex are of a spiritual nature. Thus, prostitute sex is mystical. The book of Revelation calls the practices of Sodom **"spirituality."** According to the same book, this type of spirituality is found in "the great city."

Revelation 11:8, NKJV:
*And their dead bodies will lie in the street of **the great city** which **spiritually is called Sodom and Egypt,** where also our Lord was crucified.*

The text above calls out the great city, but it does not give a name. The great city is also called Babylon[1] (which is very significant, and the importance will be

---

[1] Note: I am aware that some define this "great city" as Jerusalem. One should also research the word "where" as to how it is translated in other verses in the Bible.

discussed in a moment). However, let us look at the scriptures that show that the "great city" is Babylon, who is also the mother of harlots or porno *(Revelation 17:5).*

Revelation 16:19, NKJV:
*Now **the great city** was divided into three parts, and the cities of the nations fell. And **great Babylon** was remembered before God, to give her the cup of the wine of the fierceness of His wrath.*

Revelation 18:10, NKJV:
*Standing afar off for the fear of her torment, saying, Alas, alas, **that great city Babylon,** that mighty city! for in one hour is thy judgment come.*

Revelation 18:21, NKJV:
*And a mighty angel took up a stone like a great millstone, and cast it into the sea, saying, Thus with violence shall **that great city Babylon** be thrown down, and shall be found no more at all.*

The great city is Babylon. Her spirituality is as Sodom *(Ezekiel 16:49-0).* This indicates that the spirituality of the last days will be full of sexual perversion. Spirituality means: "of spirit", or belonging to spirit." Thus, the sexuality of Sodom is of a spirit. As stated before, Babylon the great city is equated with the spirituality of Sodom. Thus, Babylon is the spiritual source for bad sex, and she is a spiritual entity. Do you see it?

Revelation 17:1, NKJV:
Then one of the seven angels who had the seven bowls came and talked with me, saying to me, **"Come, I will show you the judgment of the great harlot who sits on many waters.**

Revelation 17:3, NKJV:
So he carried me away in the Spirit *into the wilderness. And I saw a woman sitting on a scarlet beast which was full of names of blasphemy, having seven heads and ten horns.*

Another proof that this prostitute woman is a **spiritual** entity was the fact that John had to be **"carried...away in the Spirit."** Therefore, this woman is a **spiritual** being that flows through some of humanity, and rule over political leaders by her prostitute sex *(Revelation 17:18).* Note: women/men who use sex to rule other women/men are using an aspect of the sorcery (the potion of wine sex) of Mystery Babylon.

Many leaders, men and women, are under this influence of the potion of sex. Listen to the text again, **"And the woman whom you saw is that great city which reigns over the kings of the earth" (Revelation 17:18, NKJV).** What is one of the ways she rules? She rules these kings by prostitute sex (among others things): **"the kings of the earth committed fornication (Gk., acts of porno)"** with her *(Revelation 17:2, NKJV).* Babylon is also called a **"mystery."** Thus, it points to her mystic or spiritual nature again.

Revelation 17:5, NKJV:
*And on her forehead a name was written: MYSTERY, BABYLON THE GREAT, **THE MOTHER** OF HARLOTS AND OF THE ABOMINATIONS OF THE EARTH.*

Revelation 17:7, NKJV:
*But the angel said to me, "Why did you marvel? **I will tell you the mystery of the woman** and of the beast that carries her, which has the seven heads and the ten horns.*

"Mystery" in the Greek has the meaning of that which is known by the initiated. This means only those who are initiated by her act of prostitute sex will really know the depths of her sensualities. Nevertheless, there is more, the Creator also revealed mysteries to selected people through His Pure Spirit. Therefore, the Creator can give understanding of this mystery woman, so that humanity is not taken by her prostitute sex.

Nonetheless, the fact that she is mysterious shows that she is of the spiritual sort. Mystery also means secret. Thus, she operates in secret, in hidden places; (many sexual perversions are done in secret and dark places). It takes understanding beyond our finite intellect to understand the truth about this mystery woman. This understanding comes from the Creator of humanity.

There is an invisible force energizing humanity to commit prostitute sex, and a lot of people follow these acts of pornography without knowing the **source.** Babylon is the *"mother of harlots (porne—feminine)."*

Thus, this woman was the one who birthed prostitute sex, or sexual vices in the earth. She **"mothered"** pornography—all the selling of sex. If she is the mother of prostitute sex, and, she is, guess who the father is? His name is Satan. In fact Satan is a homosexual, and the father of homo sex. The same historian, John, recorded a time in history when Jesus, the Christ encountered opposition from staunch religious believers.

Jesus made various interesting replies to these people. He said, *"You do the deeds of your father."* They replied, ***"We were not born of fornication (porneias); we have one Father—God" (John 8:41).*** Jesus replied, *"You are of your father the devil" (John 8:44a).* These pretentious believers have another father—the "devil" and they also had a mother—Babylon, the mother of harlots (lit., porne)—because Jesus implied that they were born of a fornicator named Satan.

Therefore, Babylon mothered prostitute sex in humanity. Therefore, the mother of all pornographic business in the world came from this mystic woman called Mystery Babylon. Now **"mother"** is from the Greek "meter" the counterpart of "father", Greek **"pater."** One of the definitions of **"father"** is **source** (Merriam-Webster).

Thus, if the **"father"** is the **male source,** then the **"mother"** is the **female source.**

In other words, Mystery Babylon is the mother, **the feminine source, of prostitute sex** and this kind of sex can make you drunk. Babylon is also called, *"the great harlot" (Revelation 17:1; 19:2).* Again, harlot means porno. Thus, this woman is personified as "porn" herself. She is **"the great porne."** She is porne! The only thing that comes from her is pornography— prostitute sex, the prostitute sex that is toxic to the mind and body of humankind. Babylon's prostitute sex is so full of pleasure that she causes her pupils to give it up for free.

Ezekiel 16:34, NKJV:
*You are the opposite of other women in your harlotry, because no one solicited you to be a harlot. In that you gave payment but **no payment was given you, therefore you are the opposite.** "*

Another historian studied the actions of harlotry and recorded his result with the help of the Creator. The Lord said a woman who gives up herself at no cost is **"opposite"** from a harlot who sells sex. I remember reading this one day, and I heard the Lord's voice in me say, *"anyone who gives up sex for free is **worse** than a harlot."* I also heard, *"at least a harlot gets paid."* In fact, both types of harlotry are bad. However, the woman or man who gives himself or herself up for free is worse than a whore who is paid. At least the whore is getting paid. Now, I am not advocating selling your body. On the contrary, keep yourself clan.

This is what the Creator was saying in Ezekiel. In the days of Ezekiel, Israel was indulging in prostitute sex. Except the harlots of that era were "giving money" for sex, rather than being paid for sex. The same is done today. Women and men alike **"give"** their own **"payment"** for prostitute sex. In other words, just to have some sex, they will pay for the hotel, rent the car, buy the wine, etc. This is prostitute sex. The Creator calls them **"opposite."** It is worse to give up your body to a person freely.

I regularly say to the single ladies, "You have something so valuable that men pay money for it. If your body is so valuable, keep it for your husband. Tell him (your date) he has to wait." I explain to the ladies that their bodies are one of the many things they give to their husband. For males and females; let it be your spouse who enjoys you freely. There are two types of harlots (male and female) on the earth.

One person gives sex free and the second gives sex for money. Both of these vices are prostitute sex. Even though both are works of prostitute sex, both devalue the body, but the one who gives it up at no cost is the worse. Note: I repeat, this does not mean that it is okay to sell your body. That means that many who look down on prostitutes are in worse shape than the prostitutes they despise. How can a person condemn a prostitute when prostitutes are smarter than the ones who gives their bodies at no cost?

In fact, those who give sex for free are just as drunk as the ones who give it for a price. *"For **all** the nations have drunk of the wine of the wrath (lit., passion) of her fornication ...." (Revelation 18:3).* Therefore, whether you give sex for free or for money, you are still being intoxicated with the wine of the passions of Babylon's prostitute sex.

Prostitute sex devalues .... Free sex devalues more .... It is not too

Same sex

Same sex—I remember a young man whom I counseled years a go in North Carolina. He stated to me that sex with another male "feels right."

It is unnatural and against human nature, for a man not to desire a woman. It is against growth for a woman not to desire a man. Same sex, according to history, is against physical activity, physical in the original sense of the Greek word for "physical"—"produce by nature", or "inborn." Today, the most popular belief is that same sex orientation is birthed in the victims. However, I propose an alternative. There is no gene that indicates homosexuality.

Children become what their parents "are", not necessarily what their parents "say." A good example of this is: a parent may say to a child, "It is not good to smoke." However, the parent smokes. Most of the times, the child may become what that parent does, smoke, in spite of their parent's words—"do not smoke." In like manner, children grow up to become what their parent/guardians do in secret.

The fact that they grow up with parents with secret sexual sins (bisexuality, homosexuality, lesbianism, etc), the child will think that same sex orientation is "produced by nature" or "inborn." This is the reason when the child asks the parents, "What is your opinion about same sex in other people?" The parent may reply, "If a person chooses to practice same sex, which is his/her choice." In other words, the parent cannot speak against it, because he/she is doing the same thing in private.

Thus, the parents answer may give the green light to the thought that the child has been wrestling with internally, "Is same sex okay?" This internal question was a result of the environment that he/she was living in. In other words, the spiritual attitude that motivated the parents is now cultivating another generation to continue same sex relations. If you want to know why same sex desires are so appealing to you, sometimes the answer is in the persons who raised you.

You were not born that way! You can become what people are (internal character), not necessarily what people say (external expression). That is, the secret practices of the parents'/guardians' lives have now been imparted to children, unknowingly. I met a gentleman who related to me that one of his children (his son) has a problem with "running up to women and grabbing their chest."

He also stated that he did not know where his son got this behavior. He indicated that he disciplines his son, but his son still feels on women. Later, I found out from this same gentleman that he [the father] has a collection of porno magazines and videos which he [the father] indulges in, heavily. This fact is the key to his son's continual misbehavior, even though the child is being disciplined. The child is not doing what the father says, "do not feel on women." The child is doing what the father practices in secret. Children are influenced by what the parents practice.

Same sex is transferred in similar ways. People are not necessarily created to prefer sex with the same gender. It can be imparted to children (inside the womb or outside the womb). Same sex is against physics in the sense that matter and energy are related to interaction. Physics is also the study of the mechanics of things—how do things work. Sexuality has a legal mechanics to its function.

Romans 1:26-27, NKJV:

[26] *For this reason God gave them up to vile passions. For even their women exchanged the **natural (Gk., physical or physics)** use for what is against **nature (Gk., growth).** [27] Likewise also the men, leaving the **natural (Gk., physical or physics)** use of the woman, burned in their lust for one another, men **with (lit., in)** men committing what is shameful, and receiving in themselves the penalty of their error which was due.*

The females **exchanged** the physical use of their body for that which is against growth. Physically, the female was created for the male. The male has the "growth" for the female. The female has the "growth" for men. The "physical growth" of the female was not made for another female. The "physical growth" of the male was not designed for another male. It does not fit. The woman has no "growth"—penis—for penetration, and the male was not made with a vagina to receive another male. Male and females are the opposite. Male and female are not the same opposite. They are opposites. The female has growth in the chest area that is part of her femininity. The male does not have the same type of growth in the chest area, which displays part of his masculinity.

The word **"against"** in *Romans 1:26* above also means **"near"** in the Greek. Thus, the phrase could also read, their women exchanged the **natural (Gk., physical or physics)** use for what is **"near"** nature. "Near nature" means that the women also had sex that was near nature. That is, they may have performed anal sex. This sexuality is near the nature—physical function—of the female. This form of sexuality is near nature, not the actual physical design. The Hebrew definition for female means: to puncture.

However, they are **not** to be punctured in the anus. They are to be, so to speak, punctured in the vagina during covenant sex, in marriage. Those who practice same sex are opposite. The women **"exchange" (lit., make different)** their physical use to other uses—anal sex, same sex, apparatus sex, etc. The male, however, **"leaving (lit., to send away)"** the physical use of the women. There are men who send away the woman for other men. They go up to seven month without sex with their spouses, because they are having same sex with other males, or sex with other women. If your husband/wife likes to go too long (months) without intercourse, something may be unnatural—you should question the motive. It is unnatural for a male not to want a female. It is unnatural for a female not to desire a male. At the same time, I am not advocating excessive sex.

Same sex also is a dysfunction of physics as stated in Verse 26. The mechanics of same sex does not work. The physical properties of same sex do not work. The "energy" of same sex and the "matter" of same sex have no real relationship. There is no spiritual satisfaction in the parties involved, only temporal pleasure. The physical may be satisfied; yet, the spiritual longs for true sexual communion. No matter how much same sex may "feel right", deep, deep on the inside, it is against the created nature of your being and body.

The body, through deceases; pains from abnormal use; rectum malfunction; vaginal pain, etc tells "your-story," or, should I say, "your history." Historically, same sex began in the invisible and then manifested in the visible. Life is like a symmetric object with a line of axis in the middle. On one side of the axis—the line between visible and invisible—there is a spiritual reality. On the other side of the axis, there is a symmetric natural reality. In other words, same sex is a mirror exposure of something that happened historically in the invisible. Same sex is "the lie."

Romans 1:24-25, NKJV:
[24] *Therefore God also gave them up to uncleanness, in the lusts of their hearts, to dishonor their bodies among themselves,* [25] *who exchanged the truth of God for* **the lie,** *and worshiped and served the creature rather than the Creator, who is blessed forever. Amen.*

John 8:44-45, NKJV:
You are of your father the devil, and the desires of your father you want to do. He was a murderer from the beginning, and does not stand in the truth, because there is no truth in him. When he speaks **a (Gk., the) lie,** *he speaks from his own resources, for he is a liar and the* **father** *of it.*

The devil **fathered** some things. One of them is "the lie." However, what is the lie? The foremost reason same sex is manifested in the natural has to do with the lie that was fathered by Satan. Historically, humans were famous for worshipping "creatures", including human creatures and animal creatures. This is the lie. Worshiping the creature instead of The Creator is the lie. Worshipping the creature instead of the Creator is same sex. We call it homosexuality. Allow me to explain.

Satan fathered the lie. Thus, according to *Romans 1:25,* he is the source of creature (animal) admiration. Jesus stated that *"he [Satan] speaks the lie."* In other words, he [Satan] caused other angels—creatures—to worship him [a creature]. God says that creature worshipping creature is the lie. The same God also states that creature worshipping creature results in same sex. In other words, when the other created beings worshipped Satan, a created being, in God's opinion, it was the same as a homosexual act.

In the world today men worship men, women worship women, men worship women and women worship men. Men worship women's body parts—buttocks, thighs, faces, noses, eye colors, hair, breast, etc. Women worship men's body parts. Humans worship human basketball players, human football players, human soccer players, human tennis players, human hockey players, human historical figures, and men's mind. The arenas are filled with the indulgers. The result of this kind of male and female worship is sexual sin.

Categorically, athletes and famous people whom other humans worship fall into sexual sins. They indulge in all manner of dishonorable sex that ranges from adultery sex to same sex. Listen to the news or read carefully the news. The reason for this kind of human behavior is that mankind refused to retain the Creator in their minds. Instead, humanity worships the very thing that they are—a created being. Man was created to worship the Creator, not the creature. Creature worshipping creature is same sex.

The word homosexuality has a Greek etymology. **"Homo"** is a Greek word that means **"same." "Sex"** means a division of gender or species. Satan is a species of creature. We call them angels. Angel species worshiping angel species is a homosexual act. They are the **SAME** creature **SPECIES** worshiping each other. In other words, the beauty of man's performance has become the idol of mankind. This is what the Creator calls "the lie." God's heart is crushed according to the Holy Writ.

The sign that there is an abundance of creature worship on the earth is the prevalence and acceptance of same sex behavior. Men have made their own image a god. Man has made the image of animal—a creature—a god. Most animals were made to eat and to have fun with. They were not made to be worshipped. Man was made to dominate the animal kingdom, not to worship creatures. The image of beasts and the image of men are now the idols of this age. The result is the uncleanness of same sex.

All of the manifestation of same sex is a result of the spirit of Satan causing creature worship. Satan went against God's physics when he caused this lie. Satan and mankind gave their back to God; thus, God gave their backs to one another—men behind men, women behind women. Creature worshipping creature was not the spiritual or physical relationship that God intended. His intent **is** for creature to worship Creator. The physics of this kind of worship always works.

"Worship the Creator lest He be angry …."

Marriage sex

Appropriate sexuality satisfies a debt—Marriage sex

Marriage adds value to all who participate in it. In marriage a debt is satisfied. This reality is demonstrated in humanity. The worth of women is so valuable that men pay money to sleep with them. Thus, sex with a woman is valuable. In addition, it is innate in man to realize that sex has value. Mankind naturally puts value on sex.

Hebrews 13:4, NJKV:
*"Marriage is **honorable (lit., valuable) among (Gk., in)** all, and the bed undefiled...."*

Marriage is "valuable." The Greek for honorable also mean "money paid." This is strange, marriage is money paid? Thus, there is a payment involved in marriage. In fact, marriage satisfies a debt. Marriage satisfies a debt "in" all—those who are partakers in it. This value or money paid is then linked to the "bed." Here it is again.

"Marriage", "money paid" or "value" is linked to the "bed." Remember, men and woman pay money for sex or going to bed with a person for the pleasure of touch. This value placed on sex should only be satisfied in marriage sex. True honor (value) in sex is only realized in marriage—*"marriage is honorable ...."* Sex outside of marriage—prostitute sex—devalues humanity.

With prostitute sex the value that is to bring honor now brings dishonor. That is why most prostitutes (male and female) have serious self esteem issues. The participants—the buyer and seller—usually have very low self esteem. He/She for the most part is trying to add value to their lives. The buyer wants to have the value of sex. The seller is placing value on his/her body. However, the value added to the money paid is temporary, because the participants are not truly committed to living together in marriage. Marriage sex is permanent.

In other words, when sex is paid in marriage there is a sense of worth. The husband adds value to the wife— her total person. The wife adds value to the husband— spirit, soul and body. The bed is also "undefiled" in marriage. This means there is cleanness to marriage sex that comes with the honor given to the undefiled marriage bed.

Conversely, there is a sense of defilement that comes along with sex outside of marriage. This could be why some men and women who commit sex outside of marriage sometimes take natural baths to try to scrub the spiritual uncleanness off their bodies. The body is defiled by devaluation. In fact, it is only in marriage that the debt of adding value to each other can be satisfied; and this satisfaction of debt is directly linked to sex.

1 Corinthians 7:2-3, NKJV

² *Nevertheless, because of sexual immorality, let each man have his own wife, and let each woman have her own husband.* ³ *Let the husband* **render** *to his wife the* **affection due** *her, and likewise also the wife to her husband.*

The historical definitions of the highlighted words above are as follow: **Due** is defined as "a sum owed" and "indebtedness." **"Render"** and **"affection"** also mean "payment to be made", "to pay." The Greek structure for part of the text above may also read as such: Let the husband **pay** to his wife the **payment (of) sum owed** to her. This text, if read in context, was encouraging people not to participate in prostitute sex (sexual immorality), but to marry a husband or wife to satisfy the debt of sexual desires in the value of marriage sex.

In this age a lot of marriages are in sexual debt. In counsel with couples we have heard of cases where the wife withholds sex from the husband and the husband refuses to participate in regular sex with his wife. This could be linked to the fact that he/she may have extra marital relationships. I understand that some people are dysfunctional sexually because of rape, incest, etc. Healing has to take place in all cases. However, I have heard of men who go up to seven months without sex with their wives. They do not realize that they are indebted to their spouse. This is one of the reasons for adultery. The spouse has a void—a debt that has to be paid.

If the debt of marriage sex is not satisfied, there will be unfaithfulness. The spouse who was devalued will seek to be valued with someone else. However, in spite of the difficulties adultery sex must not be engaged in. In the Word of God, there is a safety net for those who are victims of spouses who desire to commit adultery or who have committed adultery.

1 Corinthians 7:4, NKJV:
The wife does not have authority over her own body, but the husband does. And likewise the husband does not have authority over his own body, but the wife does.

The husband has authority over the wife's body and the wife has authority over the husband's body. Legal rights can be exercised over the bodies of each other. This means that if a husband is committing or trying to commit adultery, the wife can pray that his penis does not erect. She can pray that he does not perform sexually. Why? He is giving her value of marriage sex to another.

The same is true for a husband with an unfaithful wife. He can pray that she never gets vaginally moist in her unfaithfulness. He can pray that the scent of the act be repulsive. For those who do not know, there is a scent that is unique to a couple *(Song 1:12; Song 7:8).*

Every couple has an attractive scent that cannot be denied. God can cause the aroma of an adulterous spouse to be foul to frustrate the act. The indebtedness of marriage sex must be paid. It is a law. However, it must only be satisfied in marriage sex.

The woman has a value the man wants. It is called sex and respect. The man has a value the woman wants. It is called the value of his loving affection towards her and brooding over her with warmth. He needs the satisfaction of the value of sex from her, primarily, and he needs the satisfaction of affection, secondarily. Primarily, she needs his satisfaction of strengthening her weakness through his valuing her. She needs sex, secondarily. Both debts are satisfied through value of marriage. "Marriage is valuable in all."

Marriage is supposed to add value to both parties. There is a feeling that is experienced during the wedding. This feeling has to do with value. The woman feels valuable in all her glorious apparel, because "a man" saw value (internal worth) in her to marry her. The man has a similar experience. She sees value in him to respect him as her husband. Marriage sex is the consummation of satisfying the debt. Men are called to add value to the women, even though sometimes men may act like they do not value women.

1 Peter 3:7, NKJV:
*Husbands, likewise, dwell with them with understanding, giving **honor (lit., value, money, money paid)** to the*

wife, as to the weaker vessel, and as being heirs together of the grace of life, that your prayers may not be hindered.

It is a historical fact as seen above that all ladies like to spend money. Men are supposed to give money to the wife. Wives like to shop and buy things for themselves and the home. However, the emotional part of her is more important. Value is to be added to her person. Men are very inconsistent in this area.

They are so inconsistent in this area that God had to command *"husbands ... give value"* to the spouse. Actually when a male adds value to his lady it strengthens her. The historian, Peter says to add value to her "as to the weaker vessel." Thus, giving value to the spouse builds strength. Marriage is strengthened through good words, healthy touch, relating, sex, etc.

The same is true for a man. If she is "weaker", then this also means that he is "weak." Therefore, he also needs strength from his wife. She should add value to him. This is also done through good words, respect, and marriage sex. Value will be added and debts will be satisfied. Marriage sex is important and should not be abused. Married couples should purge from their beds the devaluation caused by impure sex. This devaluation could have been brought into the marriage by those who were not virgins before marriage.

In other words, some things may have happened in sexuality before marriage that should not be practiced any longer. Some of this purging takes time. Sometimes it may take the same number of years you were living before you decide to **change your mind** to completely stop practicing certain things.

Therefore, a spouse should make it an early practice to delete any practices that cause devaluation of the body and character. I am speaking about anal sex. In addition, there may be other indulgences which do not promote healthy emotions. Yes, marriage is honorable in all and **the bed undefiled.** However, the same text says, *"but fornicators (Gk., pornos) and adulterers God will judge" (Hebrews 13:4, NKJV).*

Pornos, transliterated as, porno will be judged. Porno in Greek history has to do with selling the body for sex outside of marriage. It has to do with incest and other "kinds" of porno acts. Likewise, some of the things that were done in uncleanness will devalue marriage sex. Add more value to your marriage sex by not allowing those things which may cause uneasiness.

Husbands satisfy the debt of your wives. Give them affection of value with kind words; give them value by loving their internal character; give them your affection by esteeming them with money; and give them the payment of marriage sex. (Men should make sure their wives are pleased sexually by controlling premature ejaculations.) Wives satisfy the debt to your husband.

Give them the value of marriage sex; give them the value of appreciation for their person; give them the value of respect; add value to their positional role.

Marriage is honorable!

Anger sex

Anger sex—some people who indulge in homosexual/lesbian bashing from rage were violated, themselves ....

One of the foremost causes of anger in mankind today is from sexual molestation. Fathers violate their daughters; fathers violate their sons and mothers violate their sons; mothers violate their daughters. Brothers violate their sisters, sisters their brothers, Fathers-in-law, and other-in-laws may be involved. Men violate boys; women violate girls. Besides incest, there is rape, etc. These violations and others like these are a source of anger. Some forms of sex are filled with anger. I call it anger sex.

Growing up, I was very angry at homosexuals to the point of not wanting to be associated with them. I despised them, and sometimes wanted to hit them (if they came near me). Some abusers and the exploited emit defilement unconsciously—that is the victim's defilement may say to others, "Hit me." When someone is abused, there is a non-visible attitude that some carry around in themselves that emit the words, "Hit me" or "Abuse me." Thus, some people who are sexually perverted could be attacked for what appears to be no apparent reason. As a child, I did not realize <u>why</u> I was so angry with sexual violators until I got a little older. In my sub-conscience, I was angry at the reality that violation (unknowingly and knowingly) took place when I was a little boy. Because of violation, again knowingly and unknowingly, anger was used as a defense mechanism. Why? Anger was the protection from the potential of being violated again. I was angry; because deep inside, there was a hate for impure sexuality. Today, I can say that I no longer carry that mind-set of hate.

The same is true for most today. Humanity is angry with their own person, because they either violated others, or they felt violated by others. In other words, some blame themselves for being violated when indeed it was not their fault. Society is angry and lashing out against those who have different sexual orientation (i.e. gays, lesbians, rapist, etc). In addition, there are those who are angry because they were violated unwillingly. The point is this: Anger is associated with impure sex, and this anger sex imparts furious passion.

Revelation 18:2-3, NKJV:
*"[2] ...Babylon the great is fallen, is fallen, and has become a dwelling place of demons, a prison for every foul spirit, and a cage for every unclean and hated bird! [3] For all the nations have drunk of the wine of the **wrath of her fornication** ...."*

There is a **"wrath"** associated with **"fornication."** As stated before, fornication is the Greek word translated as porno from which derives the English word pornography. Thus, anger is associated with sexual sins.

Sometimes when siblings have intense hate and anger for each other, it is because there is some kind of irregular sexual behavior. The body hates to be violated and will tell on the involved by emotional displays and body language. Before we discuss the wrath of sexual sins, allow me to establish that fact that there are "kinds" of sexual immorality. Greek history tells us that in their society there were different manifestations of sexual sins. In the case I am about to cite it was a form of sexuality that caused anger—anger sex.

1 Corinthians 5:1, NKJV:
*It is actually reported that there is **sexual immorality (or porno)** among you, and **such** sexual immorality as is not even named among the Gentiles--that a man has his father's wife!*

1 Corinthians 5:1, NASU:
*It is actually reported that there is immorality among you, and immorality of **such a kind** as does not exist even among the Gentiles, that someone has his father's wife.*

There are different **kinds** of sexual sins as a man sleeping with his father's wife, daughters with brothers, etc. In other words, there are different "kinds" of porno sins, and sleeping with ones father's wife is one of the kinds of porno. According to the book of Revelation, it is linked to anger sex.

"Sexual immorality" in the text above is the same word for fornication in *Revelation 18:3.* In *Revelation 18,* porno (fornication, sexual immorality, incest, harlotry, etc—see Strong's Lexicon # 4203) is linked to anger. Thus, this **"kind"** of porno is also linked with anger *(see II Corinthians 7:8-11).* All porno is directly linked to anger. Some think that porno only has to do with magazines and X-rated movies. This is not true.

Any kind of sex outside of marriage sex is porno sex. Sleeping with someone's mother is porno sex. Incest is porno sex. Same sex is porno sex, and, according to the Creator, decadent sex causes anger. As stated earlier in this book, recently I gave a seminar on porno sex. The next day I was given a copy of a newspaper that stated how a military man killed his wife over pornography (The Sun: Tuesday, Oct 1, 2003, Page 5B).

Revelation 18:3 states that Mystical Babylon causes all nations to drink the wine of her **sexual anger.** The newspaper, referenced above, also recorded a present historical event which demonstrates that anger is associated with porno. Defilements are attached to porno, one of which is called anger. The result is anger sex—sexuality which involves anger. The participants are angry with themselves. The participants are angry with their partners. If you say you are not angry because of sexual violation, you are probably possessed with the spirit of porno. You are out of touch with your deep, deep feelings. You may be the abuser, or very calloused from abnormal use of sex.

The reality of who you are is realized when you get by yourself at night upon your bed and think about the practices of your life; and you find yourself crying deep, deep on the inside. This is when the reality of your being angry with yourself and/or others is activated. The result of this is usually drunkenness as the hate of self gets deeper. **(There is a way out ...)** There is a nature built in the bodies of mankind to rebel against sex that causes anger. Most vices are done apart from the body. Nevertheless, a person who commits porno—anger sex—sin against his/her own body. **Your body is saying, "STOP, STOP, and STOP!"**

I stated above how angry I was that I was violated. To solidify this truth further there are other historical facts. There was great king (David) who had many sons and daughters. One of his sons wrongly desired his sister. The son eventually, by schemes, forced himself on his sister. The irony of the event is that she, the violated, was not the first to manifest anger. The violator was the first to express anger and hate towards the person he violated. Impure sex in all its forms generates anger in the abusers. This anger really is hurtful. Especially, when anger associated with sex is generated towards the victim.

> ### 2 Samuel 13:1-15, NKJV:
> *[1] After this Absalom the **son of David** had a lovely **sister**, whose name was Tamar; and Amnon **the son of David loved her**. [2] Amnon was so*

distressed over his sister Tamar that he became sick; for she was a virgin. And it was improper for Amnon to do anything to her. ³ But Amnon had a friend whose name was Jonadab the son of Shimeah, David's brother. Now Jonadab was a very crafty man. ⁴ And he said to him, "Why are you, the king's son, becoming thinner day after day? Will you not tell me?" Amnon said to him, "I love Tamar, my brother Absalom's sister." ⁵ So Jonadab said to him, "Lie down on your bed and pretend to be ill. And when your father comes to see you, say to him, 'Please let my sister Tamar come and give me food, and prepare the food in my sight, that I may see it and eat it from her hand.' " ⁶ Then Amnon lay down and pretended to be ill; and when the king came to see him, Amnon said to the king, "Please let Tamar my sister come and make a couple of cakes for me in my sight, that I may eat from her hand." ⁷ And David sent home to Tamar, saying, "Now go to your brother Amnon's house, and prepare food for him." ⁸ So Tamar went to her brother Amnon's house; and he was lying down. Then she took flour and kneaded it, made cakes in his sight, and baked the cakes. ⁹ And she took the pan and placed them out before him, but he refused to eat. Then Amnon said, "Have everyone go out from me." And they all went out from him. ¹⁰ Then Amnon said to Tamar, "Bring the food into the bedroom, that I may eat from your hand." And Tamar took the cakes which she had made, and brought them to Amnon her *brother in the bedroom. ^{11} Now when she had brought them to him to eat, he took hold of her and said to her, "Come, lie with me, my sister." ^{12} And she answered him, "No, my brother, do not force me, for no such thing should be done in Israel. Do not do this disgraceful thing! ^{13} And I, where could I take my shame? And as for you, you would be like one of the fools in Israel. Now therefore, please speak to the king; for he will not withhold me from you." ^{14} However, he would not heed her voice;* **and being stronger than she, he forced her and lay with her.** ^{15} *Then Amnon* **hated** *her exceedingly, so that the hatred with which he hated her was greater than the love with which he had loved her. And Amnon said to her, "Arise, be gone!"*

This is a profound event. After Amnon raped his own sister, he then "hated" her, and kicked her out of the place where he defiled her. Can you imagine the pain she felt? The defiler became angry with the defiled. The point is this: sexual immorality causes anger, especially, in rape victims. Incest causes anger. This kind of sexuality is part of anger sex. Two of Jacob's sons killed a group of men because their sister was raped by one of their associates. Their father had to curse the anger that was generated by sexual violation. Anger is directly linked to sexual sins.

There are people who try to hide with anger sex the truth that they were sexually violated. However, Revelation says that "all nations" partook of the anger of porno. Thus, most of the world has some hidden violation in their lives and they are angry. However, as stated earlier, there is a Way out.

The Way is Jesus. When one studies the genealogy of Jesus, His history is filled with sexual sinners, but it did not disqualify Him to be the Savior. If you have sexual sins in your background, ranging from you to your family history, **you are a candidate to be used by God for good.** I am not justifying the sin. I am saying that He will justify you.

Jesus' history consists of Abraham who married his half sister, Judah who had children by his son's wife, Ruth who was a Moabite—children of father and daughter incest. Solomon was born from parents of a sex crime; Rahab was a strumpet, etc, etc. The point is this: Jesus was sinless even though His historical lineage was bad. He can make you sin-free regardless of your background. In other words, God will not hold your history against you if you turn to Him through Jesus.

If you have anger sex in your background you are a candidate to be healed and used by the Creator ...

No sex

No sex is a calling. It cannot be legislated by men's rule. It is against nature to try to stop sex.

In today's human trend, sexuality is main stream. To say that one can keep himself or herself from sex is next to impossible for most men and women. The truth is: they are correct. No sex is a call; no sex is inborn. Only those who intrinsically have a nature to abstain, can. Only those who have been called to no sex can abstain. Other than those cases, it is next to impossible to stop sex once it is awakened.

Song of Solomon 2:7, NKJV:
I charge you, O daughters of Jerusalem, By the gazelles or by the does of the field, ***Do not stir up nor awaken love Until it pleases.***

There is something about sex that once it is awakened, it is difficult to abate. Solomon, a man who understood sexuality—he had 700 wives and 300 concubines—made the statement above. Do not stir nor awaken love until it pleases. The only time it [sex] pleases the Creator is marriage sex. Therefore, do not activate sex until the proper time.

This is where parental teaching—not only school—plays a role. The parent must teach sons and daughters that their sexuality is for covenant and producing children.

Parents must teach the value of the children's bodies as it relates to marriage sex.

That is, teach the children that their sexuality is too valuable to be given up for free, with the potential results of pregnancy or disease. Parents should add value to the children's sexuality. Tell them that a person is stronger when they walk independently of other people's opinion about their virginity. Teach them not to arouse sex until the proper time of marriage consummation. Teach them about the devaluation of the body that someone may have experienced when he/she started sex too early.

Many times people (male and female) activate sex prematurely, and end up in trouble—especially a girl who may just want a touch from a boyfriend The next thing she knows, she is in a sexual situation that is not in agreement with her original intent. Ladies, if you arouse sexuality in a man, it will be hard to abate. It usually goes further than you may have intended *"Do not stir up nor awaken love until it pleases."* Love is a passion that is not to be aroused until the fit time. This is why I say it is a difficult thing to abate.

Another aspect of no sex that has to be addressed is that there are those who try to cultivate no sex by scare tactics and rules. Sexuality is such a powerful drive for some that scare tactics do not work for all. The passion of sex, once it is "stirred" or "awakened," is difficult to put back to sleep. Did you know that a married woman who gets divorced, or becomes a widow feels pain in her sex organs after a period of long abstinence? Most people think that the pain of no sex for a long period is only for men. Not so!

Yet, there are many who try to use rules (Church rules) to enforce abstinence after sexuality is aroused. Alternately, society tries to use scare methods. The only enforcers of no sex are God's ways. God's ways are: develop self-worth through Jesus. It must be inborn for a person to dedicate a lifetime to no sex; and you must have been called to no sex after you committed your life to the kingdom of God. This last statement is for those who may have been sexually involved before a relationship with God, and now they want to abstain for the kingdom of heaven's sake. It is okay to abstain from sex if you wish. As long as the decision to live a life of no sex is not because someone is forcing you against your will.

Abstinence is a call. If you are not called to "no sex," it will be difficult to abstain from marriage or any type of sex. Some claim to be celibate. However, the reality is, their celibacy is mostly from the opposite sex. The same so called celibate ones are involved in acts of same sex. There are so called men of God, abstaining Christians, etc who say they are celibate, but in the dark, they sleep with other men and women. Thus, an unforced lifestyle of no sex is innate. In fact, let us look at the concept of no sex from the standpoint of its being a "call," and not something to be legislated by men's laws.

1 Corinthians 7:1, 7, 17, 20, NKJV:
*[1] Now concerning the things of which you wrote to me: It is good for a man not to touch a woman .... [7] For I wish that all men were even as I myself. But each one has his **own gift** from God, one in this manner and another in that ....[17]But as God has distributed to each one, as the Lord has **called** each one, **so let him walk**. And so I ordain in all the churches .... [20] Let each one remain in the **same calling** in which **he was called.***

The historical context of this text is in reference to abstaining from sexual sins *(1 Corinthians 7:1)*. Paul called no sex a "call" and a "gift" from God. Thus, if "no sex" is not innate, you do a disservice to your "gift" in life. Jesus said that there are men who were made eunuchs by other men *(Matthew 19:12b)*. This involves castration to impose abstinence.

He also said that there were men who made themselves eunuchs *(Mathew 19:12c)*. These persons have the fruit of self-control for no sex, and can truthfully abstain with no secret vices. However, Jesus did not start with those two statements. He said first.

Matthew 19:12a, NKJV:
*"For there are eunuchs who were **born** thus from their mother's womb...."*

This tells us that no sex is foremost inborn. Jesus was born to the lifestyle of no sex. Paul was called to the lifestyle of no sex. If you are not born to "no sex" and not called to no sex, then, do not try to live with no sex. Children are a planting of the Lord. Someone—those who are called to have children—have to have children. No sex is not for those who are not called to the lifestyle.

The reason why priests and nuns are sinning with young boys, young girls, men, and women is because they are suppressing an inborn nature. When sexuality is suppressed presumptuously there will be an explosion of sexual perversion. Now, if an adult wants to live a life of no sex, it should be one's own choice; *"and there are eunuchs **who have made themselves** eunuchs for the kingdom of heaven's sake" (Matthew 12:19c).*

Did you know that Jesus did not make anyone follow him: *"Whoever **desires**, let him take of the water of life **freely" (Revelation 22:17d).* The book of Ecclesiastes also indicates that a man will hurt his own person when he tries to rule over another man *(Ecclesiastes 8:9).* Thus, self-adjustment must be embarked upon by a person independently of a system trying to make that person abstain. "No sex" cannot be legislated. A person must realize his/her value through understanding self-worth; and they must have a reason to practice no sex. It should be for "the kingdom of heaven's sake."

Men of today say they cannot abstain for a long time. For those who are called to no sex, I have something to tell them. There is a man who abstained from sex for about five hundred years, and history served us well by telling us that the five hundred years' abstinence occurred when the "dress" of humanity did not cover as much as it did today.

In fact, in his day, there was a prevalence of angel sex and mind sex because angels were looking on the "beautiful" daughters of Adam. The man's name is Noah, and the beautiful women of his day did not tempt him. He walked in self-control. He married when it was time.

Genesis 5:32, NKJV:
*And Noah was **five hundred** years old, **and Noah begot** Shem, Ham, and Japheth.*

Genesis 6:9, NKJV states that *"Noah was a **just man**, perfect in his generations. Noah **walked** with God."* Thus, abstinence for five hundred years of no sex is possible. Be like Noah, ***"Do not stir up nor awaken love Until it pleases."*** Noah did not stir love until the pleasing time—the time of his marriage sex.

No sex may be impossible to some, but if you are called to no sex and there is an inborn desire to abstain, you can!

No sex is possible through Jesus, Do you believe …?

Wine sex

Illicit sex is a type of wine—Wine sex. Natural wine makes you sleep, and in your sleep you will do naked things ....

Revelation 17:2-3, NKJV:
*With whom the kings of the earth committed fornication, and the inhabitants of the earth were made drunk with **the wine of her fornication.***

In the historical text above we see that humankind can be intoxicated by illicit sex. Have you ever thought of that? Any **kind** of sex outside of marriage is considered a form of "wine"—the wine of fornication.

"Fornication" is from the Greek word "porneías." It originally meant one who sells his/her body for money. It also means the many forms of sex outside of marriage. There are different "kinds" of porneías. The English word **porno** also comes from this word "porneías" as can be seen in the spelling of the word **"porno."**

Thus, intoxication by illegal sex has to do with porno sex, adultery sex, incest, sex before marriage, pedophilia, etc. Yes, all illegal, sex before God, is considered as wine that can make a person drunk (filled with toxic sex). The principle is this—too much natural wine will cause a person to get drunk.

The same things apply to wine sex; it can make a person intoxicated. This sexual intoxication is caused by a mystical entity called Babylon. Babylon uses her potion of wine to sedate her victims. During this sedation, some hidden things affect the participants because of wine sex.

Proverbs 23:29-30, NKJV:
*²⁹ Who has **woe?** Who has **sorrow?** Who has **contentions?** Who has **complaints?** Who has wounds without cause? Who has **redness of eyes?** ³⁰ Those who linger long at the wine, Those who go in search of mixed wine.*

Those who linger long at the wine [of sex] will automatically receive some bad things. Wine sex causes ***"woe."*** "Woe is me for I am drunk with sex, and I do not know how to free myself." "Woe is me because God is angry at me for abusing my body." "Woe is me because I may be headed for hell and I cannot stop the madness." Do these woes sound familiar?

Wine sex causes ***"sorrow."*** Did you notice how much sorrow bad sex brings? Let us look at some of them. There is the sorrow of having children too early, the sorrow of too many mates, the sorrow of abortions, the sorrow of an abused body, the sorrow of a worn out body, the sorrow of a diseased body, and the sorrow of losing one's virginity.

Wine sex causes *"contentions."* Most of humankind who uses wine sex for pleasure is full of contentions. This was discussed in more detail in the section on anger sex. Most people who are saturated with sex are full of contentions. They are angry at themselves, and at people who are not like them. One of the reasons why there is so much contention in relationships (married or not) is because of wine sex. Next time watch the pattern. After indulging in wine sex, there could be an argument soon after.

Wine sex causes *"complaints."* "Why am I always sick?" "How come men do not stay with me very long? Why don't women stay with me?" Let me tell you a truth about how some men think. If a woman does anything and everything with a man, that man will not marry her. Men test women to see how far the man can go. If you are loose with your male partner, he will not stay long with you. If you abstain, you will attract him.

Wine sex causes *"wounds without cause."* Wine causes wounds without there being a reason. Did you ever ask the question "Why am I so hurt?" The reason is wine sex causes wounds without a cause. Except, the paradox is: the cause of the wound is because people *"linger long at the wine"*—the wine of sex. Wine causes inward wounds. So likewise, wine–sex causes wounds deep in the heart of mankind.

Wine sex causes *"redness of eyes."* 1 Thessalonians 5:7b states: *"those who get drunk are drunk at night."* A lack of sleep coupled with wine causes the redness of the eyes. Redness in the Hebrew means blearedness, to be dark (Strong's Concordance Lexicon # 2448, # 2447). A spiritual darkness comes with wine sex. The intoxicated becomes so drunk that he/she cannot see life properly.

His/her view of life becomes distorted. Sexuality becomes distorted to them also. There is no conviction in his/her heart about personal sexual perversion. Did you know that you can go *"past feeling?"* You can become numb. Adultery sex, prostitute sex, anal sex, same sex, mind sex, etc. is justified by their blindness— *"who, being **past feeling**, have given themselves over to **lewdness**, to work all uncleanness with greediness"* *(Ephesians 4:19, NJKV).*

Humanity has confused love sex with lust sex. There is a thin line between lust sex and love sex. If one is not careful, one can confuse wine sex with love. The fact is, love sex is better than wine sex. Some may say love sex is boring compared to lust sex! The reality is they fail to understand the transition from wine sex to love sex. The body by nature resists change and adjusts to the introduction of a new thing very slowly. Remember the first time you drank some alcohol, or exercised? The body reacted. It is the same when love sex is experienced in lieu of lust sex. Similar to how exercise is good for the body, and the body has to adjust to the routine of exercise, so love sex is better than wine. However, the body has to adjust to true sex.

Song of Solomon 1:2, NKJV:
*Let him kiss me with the kisses of his mouth—**For your love is better than wine**.*

Song of Solomon 4:10, NKJV:
*How fair is your love, My sister, my spouse! **How much better than wine is your love,** And the scent of your perfumes Than all spices!*

Love sex is better than wine. Better means good. Thus, when love sex is realized, the participants will feel "good" about their sexuality and about themselves. Most people do not experience this better sex, because there is a process to get there for those who were corrupted by wine sex.

One of the signs that love sex is replacing wine sex is a lack of desire even to have sex. At this point, it will appear that wine sex is better than love sex. Some will even revert to wine sex, because of the apparent lack of stimulation.

When your body is trained to do one thing, if the habit is changed, the new habit will become strange to the body. Wine sex is a **"body"** act—*"he who commits sexual immorality sins against his **own body"** (1 Corinthians 6:18b, NKJV)*. Thus, the change to love sex acts as a new law in the body. The result is; there may be no response to love sex. However, as love sex is pursued, wine sex becomes less desirable.

The trick is wine sex appears to be "better," compared to love sex. Sin has a "pleasure" with it *(Hebrews 11:25)*. Therefore, sinful sex has a pleasure in it (**"Sex Pleasures"**). These overexcited feelings tend to make wine sex feel better than love sex. One of the reasons why men ejaculate so quickly is because of an over-excited mind, relative to sex.

This over-excitement is a direct result of pornography. Thus, when true sex enters the picture one cannot perform. Why? There is no perverted stimulus present in true sex. Nevertheless, wine sex in all its so called pleasures of lust is nothing compared to love sex.

Solomon says, *"**How much better** than wine is your [Shulamite's] love."* The love of the Shulamite, Solomon's wife, is a lot better than wine. True love sex is fulfilling. Once it is realized, wine sex is no comparison. The only thing one must remember is that in the process to right sex becoming "much better" there may not be a desire for sex. Nevertheless, this is temporary. A healthy desire will eventually come back.

Remember love sex is better than wine sex ….

Oral sex

Oral sex, as it is named, is it acceptable to God (the three general opinions)?

The subject of oral sex is a very opinionated topic, with differing points of view. Thus, the text and context of this chapter were revisited to cite what are the three general opinions. God is in the business of bringing humanity closer to himself, and the scripture does not appear explicitly to discuss (approve of or disapprove of) oral sex. Thus, this author did not want to be dogmatic with just one opinion that may affect the reader in a wrong way.

Therefore, the presentation of the three beliefs is appropriate for this book. That is, one of the purposes of this book is to bring sexual repair, not sexual condemnation. I have also cited Scriptures that are generally related to the three beliefs about oral sex.

Note: the opinions are ordered randomly, and the number of scriptures cited for any opinion does not indicate that opinion is the right or wrong judgment. Some of the scriptures which are cited are in context referring to other subjects. However, in the text of the scriptures there were some general statements made that covers a broad spectrum of topics.

Opinion # 1: Oral-sex is acceptable to God

Hebrews 13:4, NKJV:
*Marriage is honorable among all, and the **bed (Greek: koitee [koy'-tay]) undefiled**; but fornicators (lit., male prostitute as venal) and adulterers God will judge.*

Genesis 2:25, NKJV:
*And they were both naked, the man and his wife, and were not **ashamed (prop; to pale [to limit,** to bound, to be deficient in color]).*

Romans 14:14, NKJV:
"I know and am convinced by the Lord Jesus that there is nothing unclean of itself ...."

Romans 14:22 NJKV:
Do you have faith? Have it to yourself before God. Happy is he who does not condemn himself in what he approves.

Opinion # 2: Oral sex is not acceptable to God

Romans 14:14, NKJV:
"... to him who considers anything to be unclean, to him it is unclean."

Romans 14:22b, NJKV:
" ... Happy is he who does not condemn himself in what he approves."

Opinion # 3: Indecision about oral sex

James 1:8, KJV:
A double minded man is unstable in all his ways.

Romans 14:23c, NJKV:
"... whatever is not from faith is sin."

Romans 14:22b, NJKV:
" ... Happy is he who does not condemn himself in what he approves."

The Lord is the Healer ...

Sex-Healing

Sex-Healing—it can take anywhere from eighteen to forty years to change a person's lifestyle

Acts 7:23-24, NKJV:
*[23] Now when he was **forty years old,** it came into his heart to visit his brethren, the children of Israel. [24] And seeing one of them suffer wrong, he defended and avenged him who was oppressed, and struck down the Egyptian.*

Acts 7:30, NKJV:
And when forty years had passed, an Angel of the Lord appeared to him in a flame of fire in a bush, in the wilderness of Mount Sinai.

Moses killed a man in the name of protecting his Israelite brothers *(Acts 7:28).* Moses' anger was so strong that he murdered. This happened at his age of forty. After he realized that the killing was not hidden, he ran from Egypt. He remained in the wilderness for another forty years before God revealed himself to Moses. It took God forty years of training to change Moses. He went from a manslayer to a protector of people.

The principle is this: The length of time that one practices sin is the same time it <u>usually</u> takes for that person to be delivered from that fault. In other words, the sexual habit that was practiced for twenty years may not stop overnight. It may take the same length of time twenty years, for that person to be freed from that vice. However, understand that some can be freed immediately, and I have seen that happen. Yet, some sexual habits may take years to stop completely. This is important to know, so as not to condemn yourself or others.

When the Lord found me at age twenty-four there were some things that stopped immediately. Yet, there were some things that I am still working on—eighteen years later (2004). I have at least another seven years to be completely healed in some areas. Some habits that were placed in my life for twenty-four years, before I decided to change, will not come out overnight. Let us look at it another way.

There is a practice in the business world to do a compilation of experiential years, rather than individual tallies. You hear a statement like: "We have a combination of 105 years of experience," the combination consists of five persons each having 21 years of experience. The idea is that each person has 21 years of experience individually. This is also true for sexuality. Say that two couples get married, and both of them got married at the age of twenty-one. Their sexuality is a combined forty-two years of past that has to be discovered (This is also true for virgins. They have durations without any experience in sexuality).

Therefore, for the twenty-one years that a spouse has lived, it could potentially[2] take another twenty-one years to heal the sexual vices, if there are any present. The sum of the spouses' years that will be needed to get to know each other could max out to forty-two years. Most sexual problems in marriages do not get resolved, because of all the years of secret sins that have not been discovered, discussed, or resolved. At the age a person decides to stop his/her sexual vices, it may take as many years to discover all that has been perverted in his/her behavior.

It may take years to find out why the anger in you (anger sex) got in your heart in the first place. The result of understanding your sexuality is you will be able to implement closure. Sex may be so full of pleasure for you that it may take years for God to curb the appetite of wrong sex that appears to be full of pleasure. It takes a long time for God to convince the mind that His goodness and kindness for release from sexual vices are true. This lengthy time to change and believe in God's release has to do with mindsets.

There is a difference between forgiveness and repentance. Forgiveness means that when you make a mistake God will release you from that sin through the blood of Jesus. Repentance, on the other hand, is the Greek word *metanoia (met-an'-oy-ah).Meta,* when it is used in the Greek, as a prefix means *'to change.' Noia*

---

[2] Relative to sexuality, one should count from the time of any adverse sexual experience. Thus, the "potential" time for sexual healing could be shorter.

means the *'mind.'* Repentance literally means 'to change the mind.' This is what God wants to do: He wants to change our mindset through the avenue of kindness and goodness which He gives to us in our mistakes.

Romans 2:4b, NKJV:
*Or do you despise the riches of His goodness, forbearance, and longsuffering, not knowing that **the goodness of God leads you to repentance?***
2 Peter 3:9, NKJV:
*The Lord is not slack concerning His promise, as some count slackness, but is longsuffering toward us, **not willing that any should perish but that all should come to repentance.***

God is willing to show you His goodness, even if it takes years, to "lead you to repentance"—a changing of the mind. He is not "willing that any (that means you) should perish." He wants all to "come to repentance." God sometimes will wait for one thousand years for someone to change his/her mind *(2 Peter 3:10).*

In other words, He is "long-suffering" with us. He will go a long way with us by showing us His goodness towards our mistakes. This is one of the reasons we must be patient with people. It may take the same duration they were practicing wrong sex to change their mind completely about their sexual past. Thus, He is L-O-N-G—S-U-F-F-E-R-I-N-G in trying to change our mind.

One of the Greek words for the healings done by Jesus is "therapeutics"—to serve as an attendant. This implies that some healing comes by therapy—Jesus serving as an attendant to the person who needs sexual healing. As stated earlier, not every healing from sexual vices is instantaneous. Some will have to be attended to with understanding for years; and this healing is directly linked to mindset. (Remember, I am not advocating sexual sins, just showing God's Grace for the sincere.)

For example: A person who sells his/her body for money (prostitute sex) will be hard to convince in his/her mind that he/she should give up that habit. First, this is their livelihood. Second, when, he/she sells the body, which means that value is given to his/her body, it will be hard to convince that person that he/she is indeed valuable without selling his/her person. In fact, most prostitutes sell their bodies because they feel that they have no value.

We call it low self-esteem. In fact as you found out earlier in this book, the fact that people pay money for sex shows the value of the individual in a negative way! This, beloved, takes years to heal sometimes, especially the emotions! A repetitive note in passing: women who are used to regular sex also feel pain (just like some men) when they have to abstain for a long time. Thus, sometimes we have to be patient with those who are being healed. Some may say that people with sexual vices have demons.

This may be true for some. However, have you noticed that some who are delivered from demons are still dysfunctional? The reason is: the heart and the mind have to be renewed and purified from bad thoughts, especially those who are involved in mind sex. The mind has to be trained not to follow the enticement of having sex loosely.

This will take a conscious effort on the part of the person trying to be healed in his/her mind. In other words, through renewing the mind in the Word of God, thought patterns can be changed. This usually takes some time to bring the desired results.

The purpose for emphasizing the long duration that it takes some people to be healed is to show that God understand the pitfalls of striving to be free. Many people condemn themselves for their mistakes and never bounce back.. However, understanding must be given about God's forbearance. God knows that when you decide to change that you will make mistakes until you finally get free.

Romans 8:33, NKJV:
Who shall bring a charge against God's elect? It is God who justifies.

Romans 5:6, NKJV:
For when we were still without strength, in due time Christ died for the ungodly.

Romans 5:7-9, NKJV:
[8]But God demonstrates His own love toward us, in that while we were still sinners, Christ died for us. [9] Much more then, having now been justified by His blood, we shall be saved from wrath through Him.

The process of sexual healing is like learning to ride a bicycle. You try your best to balance the bike in the early stage of learning. However, because of inexperience, you will fall. A good father or mother will be there for the trainee. Likewise, the Spirit of Jesus will be right by your side as you take this new journey of healthy sex. Sexual vices can be healed. So do not condemn yourself when you make a mistake.

If God cast away all who made mistakes, no one would be saved. Sexual sin in and of itself, will not disqualify a person from doing God's work. Study the lineage of Jesus. In the lineage of Jesus you will find Rahab, the whore, you will find Ruth, the Moabite (Moabites were children from incest). The man Judah (unknowingly) had children by his son's wife, Tamar. David had Solomon after an adulterous relationship in which he killed a man for his wife, Bathsheba. Solomon had sexual vices, etc., etc., etc. Does this mean that we take sexual sins lightly? The answer is no, may that attitude never be birth.

The point is this, people with sexual vices in their background are prime candidates for God to clean up their lives and make them vessels of honor. In fact, the former porno stars (the stars who get paid for porno, and the stars who give it up for free) will enter the kingdom of God before so called religious persons *(Matthew 21:31-32)*. It is not too late for you. God used Moses at the age of eighty years old after forty years of purging in the wilderness.

You may be forty or thirty saying, "It is too late for me." I think differently. He can purge you from all sexual sins, and then use you to heal others. I will say what Jesus said to some that your sins are forgiven. Go and sin no more *(John 8:11)*. And the same book also said, if you do sin, and are willing to admit your sins, he is faithful and just to forgive you of your sins, and he will also clean you from all unrighteousness *(1 John 1:9)*. You can go to God at this very moment and talk with Him.

You do not have to be formal, just be yourself. You may even sound strange to yourself, and that is okay. The first step is going to God through Jesus Christ. Second, you will need the confirmation of a human. Every one of us can go to God for healing and forgiveness of sexual sins. However, as humans, we must also confess (i.e. discuss sexual hurts, vices, etc.) to a trusted person. As humans we still feel unacceptable until someone (man or woman) on earth loves us—unconditionally—after we have discussed our feelings. The reason why humanity with sexual healing is not healed completely is because humanity has no "friend" with whom to discuss their hurts. A human touch/involvement is very important in the process of healing.

James 5:16, NJKV:
Confess your trespasses to one another, and pray for one another, that you may be healed.

Some have gone overboard and say that we should not confess to a man. However, there are issues in people's lives still unresolved because there is no one to talk to. (Sex is just one of those issues.) A writer, James, indicated in *James 5:16, "Confess ... to one another."* He did not stop there. He also stated, *"... pray for one another."* Why must we confess to a human? First, the person that we open up to (confess to) must pray for us.

Then, the sexual healing comes. This is as we unconditionally love the one who opens his or her heart for healing. As James put it, *"Confess your trespass ... that you may be healed."* Do you see this? How many children want to talk to Daddy and/or Mommy and cannot? Yet, they go all their lives full of internal sickness from sexual sins which, willingly or unwillingly, occurred. They have no one to confess to in order to bring closure.

For example, per the verse cited earlier, humanity is also involved in the healing process. Sexual healing occurs as human beings love those who are in need without the process becoming perverted. There are men of God and women of God on the earth who will not abuse people in their sexual vulnerability. Jesus met a woman at a well who may have had sexual problem in her life *(John 4)*. The women at the well had five husbands, and the sixth man she was with was not her husband. Jesus carefully developed a dialogue with her, and she acknowledged her situation.

There was such a healing that took place in her through dialogue with The Man, she ran to the village and said, *"Come see a Man ..."* Confession to a person and prayer through Jesus are powerful in healing sexual hurts. Sex is not a bad thing. Sex is God's creation. He created man and woman to procreate, so let us not make it foul. Do not stir sex until the proper time. Marriage sex is the proper occasion.

In closing, the pain of healing is sometimes confused with the pain of hurt. You are not beyond sexual repair; therefore, endure the pain as the Lord our Healer completes His work in us.

ABOUT THE AUTHOR: *Donald Peart is married to Judith Peart. They are the parents of five children. He is the founder of* **Eagle-Flight Training Center, Intl.** *Donald and Judith Peart has been involved in ministry since 1986. He has a Bachelor of Science in Civil Engineering and an Associate Degree in General Studies. Donald Peart also teaches seminars on The Mega-Vision of Jesus, sexuality, the mark of the beast, the beast, why Satan hates women, etc...*

Other Books

Sexual Healing, By Judith Peart, <u>FOREWORD:</u> "Your hearts will be touched, your feelings, and emotions challenged as you read this book … Thank you Judith for your courage and transparency to help others as the Holy Spirit has helped you. Freely you have received. Freely you have given" (Dr. Sandra Phillips Hayden).

Sex-Pleasures, By Donald Peart: You are not beyond sexual repair. This book deals with topics like: "Mind sex—it has been happening for millenniums. Today, we call it wet-dreams" (Excerpt). "Sex is so valuable that men pay money for it—Prostitute sex. But, those who give sex for free are worse than strumpets—what then is Prostitute sex" (Excerpt)? This book is for the mature and those who have a difficult time being healed from sexual abuse.

The Last Hour, The First Hour, The Forty-Second Generation, By Donald Peart: This book explores the book of Revelations, the book of Daniel, the Gospels, and so on to unveil an understanding concerning the last hour, the first hour and God's hour relative to Jesus, His Church and the end of ages.

"…the false prophet …," Volume 2.1, By Donald Peart: This volume is a comprehensive instruction booklet that prophesies against "the false prophet," which is a spirit, is also known as "another beast."

EAGLE-FLIGHT TRAINING CENTER, INTL
P. O. Box 1041, Randallstown, MD 21133
1-877-843-8368